MW01013263

THE SATURDAY EVENI
CHRISTMAS
TREASURY

CLASSIC READY-TO-FRAME PRINTS AND COLORING PAGES

RENDERED FOR COLORING BY MARTY NOBLE

DOVER PUBLICATIONS, INC.
MINEOLA, NEW YORK

This special Christmas treasury includes thirty full-color, ready-to-frame prints of nostalgic Christmas images by artists whose works graced the covers of the iconic *Saturday Evening Post* and its sister magazines. In print for nearly two hundred years, *The Saturday Evening Post* has always reflected America's lifestyle, values, and interests, with one of its most prolific times being the first half of the twentieth century. During this time, *The Saturday Evening Post* was one of the most widely circulated and popular magazines for the American middle-class family, reaching millions of homes every week with its humorous renderings of often-commonplace events. The covers selected for this delightful edition were created from 1913 to 1960 by legendary artists such as Stevan Dohanos, John Falter, Henry Hintermeister, George Hughes, J. C. Leyendecker, Richard Sargent, and Norman Rockwell, who considered *The Saturday Evening Post* the "greatest show window in America."

Also included in this holiday collection are thirty black-and-white renderings for you to color with your choice of media. Captions appear on the back of both the classic images—which are printed on a heavier paper and suitable for framing—as well as on the black-and-white drawings, and include the title, the artist who created it, and the date of publication. All pages in this holiday treasury—the original full-color prints and the renditions of the famous covers—can easily be removed from the binding.

Copyright

All illustrations © SEPS.
Licensed by Curtis Licensing, Indianapolis, Indiana.
Plates 2, 11, and 17: illustrations © Rockwell Family Agency, Inc.
Licensed by IMG Worldwide, Inc.
All rights reserved.

Bibliographical Note

The Saturday Evening Post Christmas Treasury: Classic Ready-to-Frame Prints and Coloring Pages is a new work, first published by Dover Publications, Inc., in 2017.

International Standard Book Number

ISBN-13: 978-0-486-81436-0
ISBN-10: 0-486-81436-X

Manufactured in the United States by LSC Communications
81436X03   2017
www.doverpublications.com

READY-TO-FRAME PRINTS ᴀɴᴅ COLORING PAGES

Plate 1   *Mailing Letter to Santa* by J. C. Leyendecker

Plate 2   *Christmas Trio* by Norman Rockwell

Plate 3   *Santa's Lap* by J. C. Leyendecker

Plate 4   *Hug from Santa* by J. C. Leyendecker

Plate 5   *Tobogganing* by Alan Foster

Plate 6   *Santa Up a Ladder* by J. C. Leyendecker

Plate 7   *Do Not Open Until Christmas* by Henry Hintermeister

Plate 8   *We Bin Awful Good* by Henry Hintermeister

Plate 9   *Night Before Christmas* by J. C. Leyendecker

Plate 10   *Romantic Skate* by Manning de V. Lee

Plate 11   *Santa at the Map* by Norman Rockwell

Plate 12   *Postman Soaking Feet* by J. C. Leyendecker

Plate 13   *Skiing Santa* by Keith Ward

Plate 14   *Exchange and Returns Department* by Douglas Crockwell

Plate 15   *Doggy Basket* by Charles Kaiser

Plate 16   *Tree in Town Square* by Stevan Dohanos

Plate 17   *Christmas Homecoming* by Norman Rockwell

Plate 18   *Trimming the Tree* by George Hughes

Plate 19   *Christmas at the Fire Station* by Stevan Dohanos

Plate 20   *Classroom Christmas* by John Falter

Plate 21   *Truth About Santa* by Richard Sargent

Plate 22   *More Snow?* by George Hughes

Plate 23   *Bus Stop at Christmas* by Stevan Dohanos

Plate 24   *A Wife for Christmas* by Paul Nonnast

Plate 25   *Giving Santa His Seat* by Richard Sargent

Plate 26   *Christmas Morning* by John Falter

Plate 27   *All Wrapped Up in Christmas* by Richard Sargent

Plate 28   *Christmas Thank You Notes* by George Hughes

Plate 29   *Christmas in Hiding* by George Hughes

Plate 30   *Merry Christmas from the IRS* by Benjamin Kimberly Prins

The 30 ready-to-frame color prints noted above are followed by 30 coloring pages of the same images.

PLATE 1
Mailing Letter to Santa
J. C. Leyendecker
The Saturday Evening Post cover, December 20, 1913
Illustration © SEPS. Licensed by Curtis Licensing, Indianapolis, Indiana

PLATE 2
Christmas Trio
Norman Rockwell
The Saturday Evening Post cover, December 8, 1923
Illustration © Rockwell Family Agency, Inc.

PLATE 3
Santa's Lap
J. C. Leyendecker
The Saturday Evening Post cover, December 22, 1923
Illustration © SEPS. Licensed by Curtis Licensing, Indianapolis, Indiana

CHRISTMAS

PLATE 4
Hug from Santa
J. C. Leyendecker
The Saturday Evening Post cover, December 26, 1925
Illustration © SEPS. Licensed by Curtis Licensing, Indianapolis, Indiana

PLATE 5
Tobogganing
Alan Foster
The Saturday Evening Post cover, January 7, 1928
Illustration © SEPS. Licensed by Curtis Licensing, Indianapolis, Indiana

PLATE 6
Santa Up a Ladder
J. C. Leyendecker
The Saturday Evening Post cover, December 20, 1930
Illustration © SEPS. Licensed by Curtis Licensing, Indianapolis, Indiana

PLATE 7
Do Not Open Until Christmas
Henry Hintermeister
Country Gentleman cover, December 1, 1934
Illustration © SEPS. Licensed by Curtis Licensing, Indianapolis, Indiana

Plate 8
We Bin Awful Good
Henry Hintermeister
Country Gentleman cover, December 1, 1936
Illustration © SEPS. Licensed by Curtis Licensing, Indianapolis, Indiana

PLATE 9
Night Before Christmas
J. C. Leyendecker
The Saturday Evening Post cover, December 26, 1936
Illustration © SEPS. Licensed by Curtis Licensing, Indianapolis, Indiana

PLATE 10
Romantic Skate
Manning de V. Lee
Country Gentleman cover, December 1, 1937
Illustration © SEPS. Licensed by Curtis Licensing, Indianapolis, Indiana

PLATE 11
Santa at the Map
Norman Rockwell
The Saturday Evening Post cover, December 16, 1939
Illustration © Rockwell Family Agency, Inc.

PLATE 12
Postman Soaking Feet
J. C. Leyendecker
The Saturday Evening Post cover, December 21, 1940
Illustration © SEPS. Licensed by Curtis Licensing, Indianapolis, Indiana

PLATE 13
Skiing Santa
Keith Ward
Child Life cover, December 1940
Illustration © SEPS. Licensed by Curtis Licensing, Indianapolis, Indiana

PLATE 14
Exchange and Returns Department
Douglas Crockwell
The Saturday Evening Post cover, January 11, 1941
Illustration © SEPS. Licensed by Curtis Licensing, Indianapolis, Indiana

PLATE 15
Doggy Basket
Charles Kaiser
The Saturday Evening Post cover, December 19, 1942
Illustration © SEPS. Licensed by Curtis Licensing, Indianapolis, Indiana

PLATE 16
Tree in Town Square
Stevan Dohanos
The Saturday Evening Post cover, December 4, 1948
Illustration © SEPS. Licensed by Curtis Licensing, Indianapolis, Indiana

PLATE 17
Christmas Homecoming
Norman Rockwell
The Saturday Evening Post cover, December 25, 1948
Illustration © Rockwell Family Agency, Inc.

PLATE 18
Trimming the Tree
George Hughes
The Saturday Evening Post cover, December 24, 1949
Illustration © SEPS. Licensed by Curtis Licensing, Indianapolis, Indiana

PLATE 19
Christmas at the Fire Station
Stevan Dohanos
The Saturday Evening Post cover, December 16, 1950
Illustration © SEPS. Licensed by Curtis Licensing, Indianapolis, Indiana

PLATE 20
Classroom Christmas
John Falter
The Saturday Evening Post cover, December 8, 1951
Illustration © SEPS. Licensed by Curtis Licensing, Indianapolis, Indiana

Plate 21
Truth About Santa
Richard Sargent
The Saturday Evening Post cover, December 15, 1951
Illustration © SEPS. Licensed by Curtis Licensing, Indianapolis, Indiana

PLATE 22
More Snow?
George Hughes
The Saturday Evening Post cover, December 29, 1951
Illustration © SEPS. Licensed by Curtis Licensing, Indianapolis, Indiana

PLATE 23
Bus Stop at Christmas
Stevan Dohanos
The Saturday Evening Post cover, December 13, 1952
Illustration © SEPS. Licensed by Curtis Licensing, Indianapolis, Indiana

PLATE 24
A Wife for Christmas
Paul Nonnast
Country Gentleman, December 1, 1954
Illustration © SEPS. Licensed by Curtis Licensing, Indianapolis, Indiana

PLATE 25
Giving Santa His Seat
Richard Sargent
The Saturday Evening Post cover, December 10, 1955
Illustration © SEPS. Licensed by Curtis Licensing, Indianapolis, Indiana

PLATE 26
Christmas Morning
John Falter
The Saturday Evening Post cover, December 24, 1955
Illustration © SEPS. Licensed by Curtis Licensing, Indianapolis, Indiana

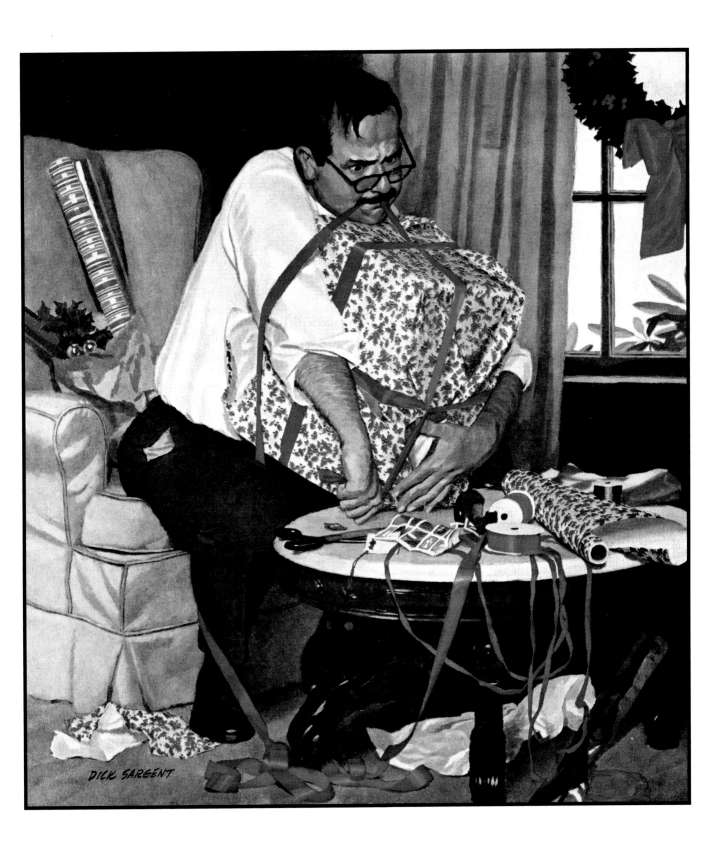

Plate 27
All Wrapped Up in Christmas
Richard Sargent
The Saturday Evening Post cover, December 19, 1959
Illustration © SEPS. Licensed by Curtis Licensing, Indianapolis, Indiana

PLATE 28
Christmas Thank You Notes
George Hughes
The Saturday Evening Post cover, January 9, 1960
Illustration © SEPS. Licensed by Curtis Licensing, Indianapolis, Indiana

PLATE 29
Christmas in Hiding
George Hughes
The Saturday Evening Post cover, December 10, 1960
Illustration © SEPS. Licensed by Curtis Licensing, Indianapolis, Indiana

PLATE 30
Merry Christmas from the IRS
Benjamin Kimberly Prins
The Saturday Evening Post cover, December 17, 1960
Illustration © SEPS. Licensed by Curtis Licensing, Indianapolis, Indiana

COLORING PAGES

PLATE 1
Mailing Letter to Santa
J. C. Leyendecker
The Saturday Evening Post cover, December 20, 1913
Illustration © SEPS. Licensed by Curtis Licensing, Indianapolis, Indiana

PLATE 2
Christmas Trio
Norman Rockwell
The Saturday Evening Post cover, December 8, 1923
Illustration © Rockwell Family Agency, Inc.

PLATE 3
Santa's Lap
J. C. Leyendecker
The Saturday Evening Post cover, December 22, 1923
Illustration © SEPS. Licensed by Curtis Licensing, Indianapolis, Indiana

C H R I S T M A S

PLATE 4
Hug from Santa
J. C. Leyendecker
The Saturday Evening Post cover, December 26, 1925
Illustration © SEPS. Licensed by Curtis Licensing, Indianapolis, Indiana

Plate 5
Tobogganing
Alan Foster
The Saturday Evening Post cover, January 7, 1928
Illustration © SEPS. Licensed by Curtis Licensing, Indianapolis, Indiana

PLATE 6
Santa Up a Ladder
J. C. Leyendecker
The Saturday Evening Post cover, December 20, 1930
Illustration © SEPS. Licensed by Curtis Licensing, Indianapolis, Indiana

PLATE 7
Do Not Open Until Christmas
Henry Hintermeister
Country Gentleman cover, December 1, 1934
Illustration © SEPS. Licensed by Curtis Licensing, Indianapolis, Indiana

PLATE 8
We Bin Awful Good
Henry Hintermeister
Country Gentleman cover, December 1, 1936
Illustration © SEPS. Licensed by Curtis Licensing, Indianapolis, Indiana

PLATE 9
Night Before Christmas
J. C. Leyendecker
The Saturday Evening Post cover, December 26, 1936
Illustration © SEPS. Licensed by Curtis Licensing, Indianapolis, Indiana

PLATE 10
Romantic Skate
Manning de V. Lee
Country Gentleman cover, December 1, 1937
Illustration © SEPS. Licensed by Curtis Licensing, Indianapolis, Indiana

P<small>LATE</small> 11
Santa at the Map
Norman Rockwell
The Saturday Evening Post cover, December 16, 1939
Illustration © Rockwell Family Agency, Inc.

PLATE 12
Postman Soaking Feet
J. C. Leyendecker
The Saturday Evening Post cover, December 21, 1940
Illustration © SEPS. Licensed by Curtis Licensing, Indianapolis, Indiana

PLATE 13
Skiing Santa
Keith Ward
Child Life cover, December 1940
Illustration © SEPS. Licensed by Curtis Licensing, Indianapolis, Indiana

PLATE 14
Exchange and Returns Department
Douglas Crockwell
The Saturday Evening Post cover, January 11, 1941
Illustration © SEPS. Licensed by Curtis Licensing, Indianapolis, Indiana

PLATE 15
Doggy Basket
Charles Kaiser
The Saturday Evening Post cover, December 19, 1942
Illustration © SEPS. Licensed by Curtis Licensing, Indianapolis, Indiana

PLATE 16
Tree in Town Square
Stevan Dohanos
The Saturday Evening Post cover, December 4, 1948
Illustration © SEPS. Licensed by Curtis Licensing, Indianapolis, Indiana

PLATE 17
Christmas Homecoming
Norman Rockwell
The Saturday Evening Post cover, December 25, 1948
Illustration © Rockwell Family Agency, Inc.

PLATE 18
Trimming the Tree
George Hughes
The Saturday Evening Post cover, December 24, 1949
Illustration © SEPS. Licensed by Curtis Licensing, Indianapolis, Indiana

Plate 19
Christmas at the Fire Station
Stevan Dohanos
The Saturday Evening Post cover, December 16, 1950
Illustration © SEPS. Licensed by Curtis Licensing, Indianapolis, Indiana

PLATE 20
Classroom Christmas
John Falter
The Saturday Evening Post cover, December 8, 1951
Illustration © SEPS. Licensed by Curtis Licensing, Indianapolis, Indiana

PLATE 21
Truth About Santa
Richard Sargent
The Saturday Evening Post cover, December 15, 1951
Illustration © SEPS. Licensed by Curtis Licensing, Indianapolis, Indiana

PLATE 22
More Snow?
George Hughes
The Saturday Evening Post cover, December 29, 1951
Illustration © SEPS. Licensed by Curtis Licensing, Indianapolis, Indiana

PLATE 23
Bus Stop at Christmas
Stevan Dohanos
The Saturday Evening Post cover, December 13, 1952
Illustration © SEPS. Licensed by Curtis Licensing, Indianapolis, Indiana

PLATE 24
A Wife for Christmas
Paul Nonnast
Country Gentleman, December 1, 1954
Illustration © SEPS. Licensed by Curtis Licensing, Indianapolis, Indiana

PLATE 25
Giving Santa His Seat
Richard Sargent
The Saturday Evening Post cover, December 10, 1955
Illustration © SEPS. Licensed by Curtis Licensing, Indianapolis, Indiana

PLATE 26
Christmas Morning
John Falter
The Saturday Evening Post cover, December 24, 1955
Illustration © SEPS. Licensed by Curtis Licensing, Indianapolis, Indiana

PLATE 27
All Wrapped Up in Christmas
Richard Sargent
The Saturday Evening Post cover, December 19, 1959
Illustration © SEPS. Licensed by Curtis Licensing, Indianapolis, Indiana

PLATE 28
Christmas Thank You Notes
George Hughes
The Saturday Evening Post cover, January 9, 1960
Illustration © SEPS. Licensed by Curtis Licensing, Indianapolis, Indiana

PLATE 29
Christmas in Hiding
George Hughes
The Saturday Evening Post cover, December 10, 1960
Illustration © SEPS. Licensed by Curtis Licensing, Indianapolis, Indiana

Plate 30
Merry Christmas from the IRS
Benjamin Kimberly Prins
The Saturday Evening Post cover, December 17, 1960
Illustration © SEPS. Licensed by Curtis Licensing, Indianapolis, Indiana